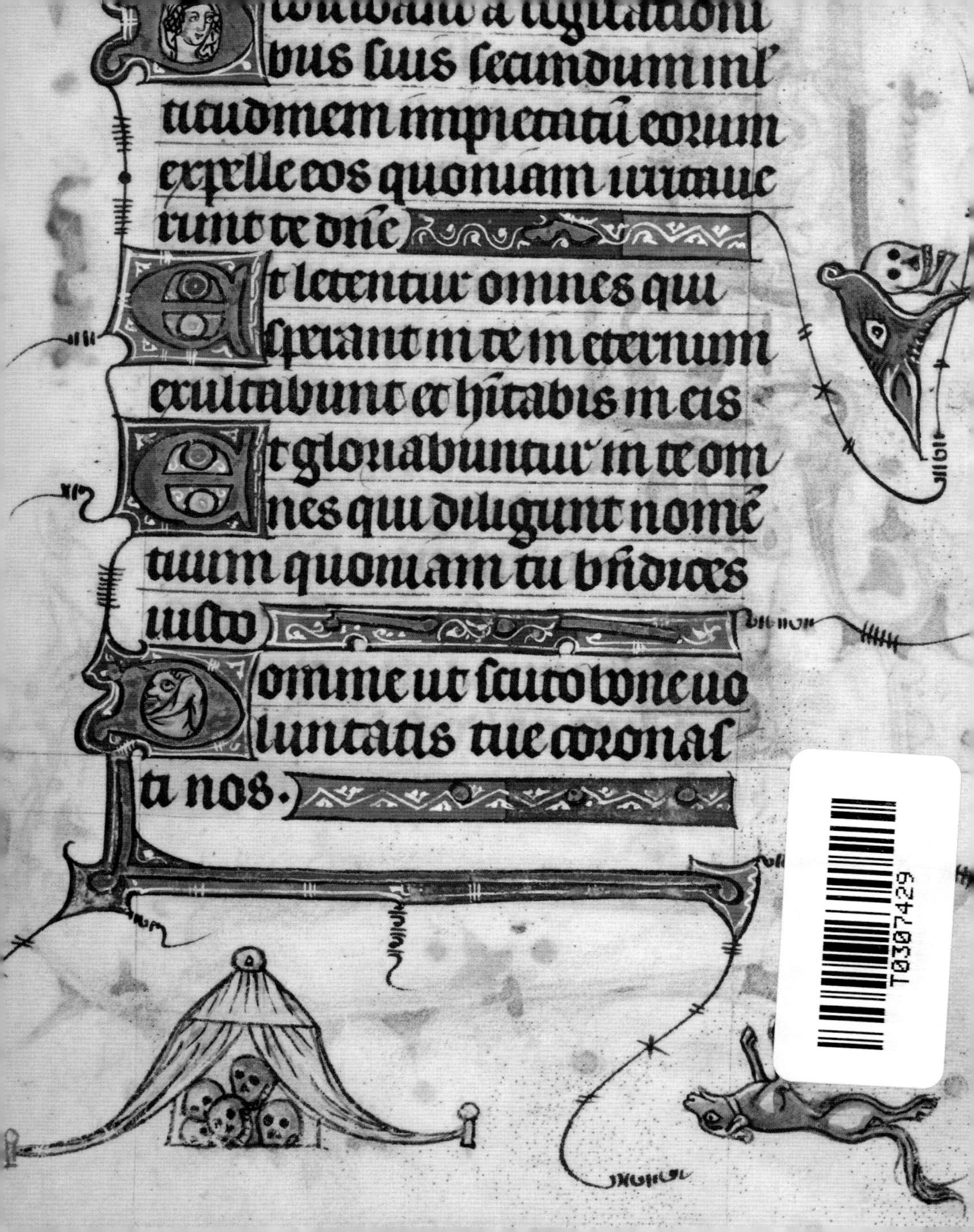
a cogitationi
bus suis secundum mul
titudinem impietatum eorum
expelle eos quoniam irritave
runt te dne
Et letentur omnes qui
sperant in te in eternum
exultabunt et habitabis in eis
Et gloriabuntur in te om
nes qui diligunt nomen
tuum quoniam tu benedices
iusto
Domine ut scuto bone vo
luntatis tue corona
ti nos.

is. ustitie dn
a letificantes cor
preceptum domini
dum illuminans
los. imor do
n sanctus perma

DOGS
✠ in Medieval Manuscripts

KATHLEEN WALKER-MEIKLE

BRITISH LIBRARY

Dogs of all kinds abound in medieval sources, from guard dogs to hunting hounds to cosseted lapdogs.

In Pierre de Beauvais's thirteenth-century bestiary, a compendium of animal lore, there are several breeds of dog listed but only two distinct types: those that hunt in the forest and those that guard houses out of love for their masters. He added that dogs can heal wounds by licking them with their tongues.

ABOVE Hunters in the forest. Hours of the Virgin, France, sixteenth century. (BL ADD. 31240 F. 5R)

OPPOSITE Men return from the hunt. Calendar Scene for November. The Golf Book. Hours of the Virgin, Flanders, sixteenth century. (BL ADD. 24098 F. 28V)

John Caius's *On English Dogges* (1570) lists a huge variety. He describes game dogs, dividing them into hunting dogs (harrier, terrier, bloodhound, greyhound, lurcher, tumbler, 'gazehound' and 'stealer') and fowling dogs that hunt birds (spaniel, setter, water-spaniel and 'fisher'). He also includes lapdogs – small dogs often described as long-haired and white, that are 'chamber companions…to satisfy the delicateness of dainty dames' and 'instruments of folly for them to play and dally'. Caius also recounts the ancient tradition of pressing a small lapdog to one's chest to relieve stomach pains or weakness. Among the working dogs, Caius mentions the mastiff, the dog-keeper (a guard dog), the butcher's dog, the dog-messenger (that 'carried letters from place to place wrapped up cunningly in his leather collar'), the mooner (that barks at the moon), the water-drawer (that turns well-wheels), the tinker's cur (that carries a tinker's buckets) and assorted 'defending dogs'. Caius ends his treatise with 'mongrel and rascal' dogs, which include the warner (that only barks), the turnspit (that turns kitchen-spits) and the dancer (a performing dog).

OPPOSITE A tinker is attacked by a dog. The Luttrell Psalter, England, *c.*1325–1335. (BL ADD. 42130 F. 70V)

n euaginauerunt pecca
enderunt arcum suum.
iant pauperem ⁊ inopē:
ant rectos corde.
s eorum intret in corda
t arcus eorum confrin

The twelfth-century abbess Hildegard of Bingen noted that dogs would demonstrate love and loyalty towards a deserving owner, but if the owner or someone in the house was disloyal or a thief, dogs would growl and gnash their teeth. She also claimed that dogs could tell the future, wagging their tails cheerfully if it was good, and howling despondently if evil events were on the way.

ABOVE The constellation Canis Minor. Ptolomy's Almagest, England, 1490. (BL ARUNDEL 66 F. 44V)

OPPOSITE The author Christine de Pisan writes in her study accompanied by a small collared dog. Christine de Pisan, Various works, France, *c*.1410–*c*.1414. (BL HARLEY 4431 F. 4R) nes ee. n̄ posse.

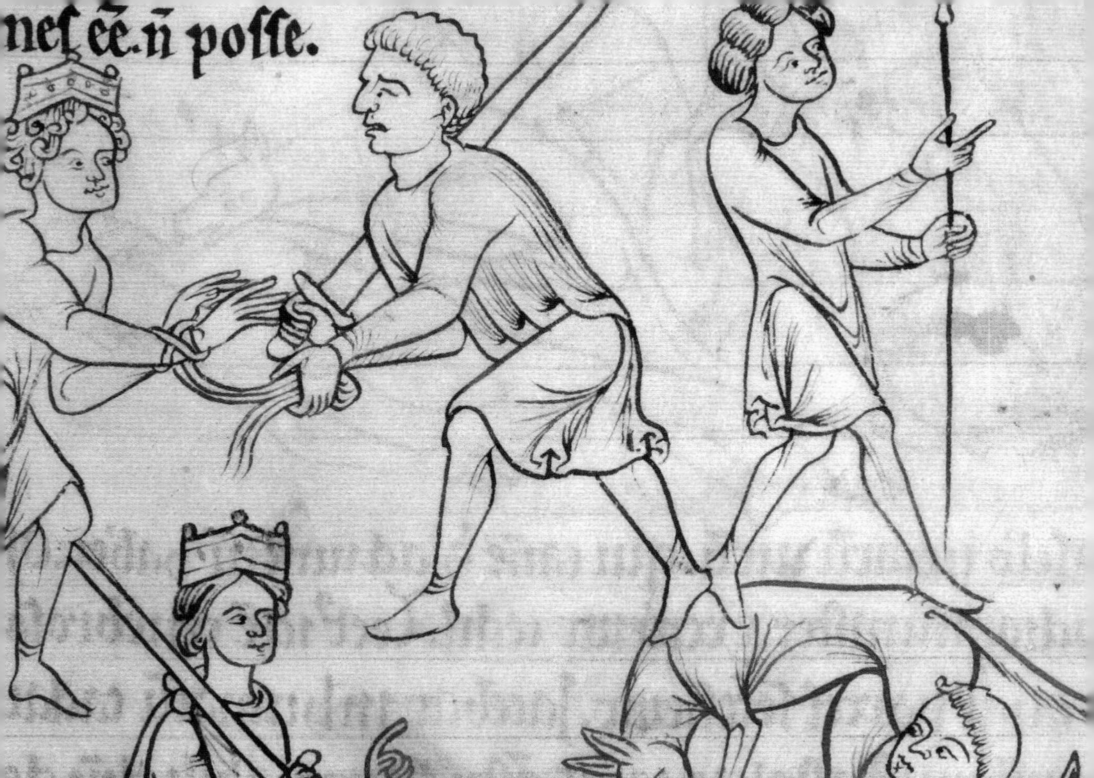

ntū suos diligere dn̄os. ut garamantē regē ab inim

na mancipatū. ducenti canes agmine facto. p media

A popular story in bestiaries came from the Roman author Pliny the Elder about a king of the Garamantes (in North Africa) who came home from exile with two hundred dogs that attacked anyone in his way.

The twelfth-century author Gerald of Wales told of a young Welshman, killed in battle against the English, whose greyhound refused to leave his master's body. The English ordered the man's body to be buried with honour, as a mark of favour towards the loyal dog.

ABOVE A hare and a dog fighting with swords. The Breviary of Renaud de Bar, France, *c*.1302–3. (BL YATES THOMPSON 8 F. 181R)

OPPOSITE The King of the Garamantes is rescued by his dogs. Bestiary, England, twelfth century. (BL ADD. 11283 F. 10R)

The tradition that dogs stay with their master's corpse is a long one. The author of *The Goodman of Paris* told how at Niort in 1373 he saw an old dog lying sadly on a grave in which his master had been buried, having been killed by the English at the battle of Chisay. The Duc de Berry witnessed how the dog refused to move from the grave and arranged for it to receive a pension of ten francs for life. The money was given to a neighbour to feed the dog.

ABOVE Dog attacks his master's murderer. Bestiary, England, second or third quarter of thirteenth century. (BL SLOANE 3544 F. 13V)

OPPOSITE Dogs hunt, a dog attacks his master's murderer and mourns over the corpse. Lapdog at bottom. Theological miscellany, including a bestiary. England, second or third quarter of thirteenth century, after *c.*1236. (BL HARLEY 3244 F. 45R)

The early seventh-century scholar St Isidore of Seville claimed that the Latin word *canis* ('dog') derived either from the Greek noun *kuon* or the Latin verb *canere* ('to sing, bark'). He wrote that dogs were cleverer than other animals, as only dogs could recognize their own names and their masters, as well as being able to guard house, hunt and remain loyal to their owner until death.

Not all medieval authors praised the loyalty of dogs. Rabanus Marus in his *On the Universe* in the ninth century pronounced that dogs only guard the houses where they are fed bread, rather than out of any innate devotion.

ABOVE Annunciation to the Shepherds. Book of Hours, France, late fifteenth or early sixteenth century. (BL ADD. 35216 F. 51V)

OPPOSITE Garden planting. Calendar scene for March. The Golf Book. Hours of the Virgin, Flanders, sixteenth century. (BL ADD. 24098 F. 20V)

The loyal dog is a popular heraldic beast. In the *Deeds of Armoury*, a fifteenth-century heraldic manual, 'a greyhound or a dog borne in arms signifies a right benign and loyal fighting man who never would leave his lord dead nor alive and is ready daily to fight for his lord'. Similarly, in the *Treatise of Arms* by Bado Aureo, composed at the end of the fourteenth century, 'A dog borne in arms represents a loyal man who will not desert his lord and master in life or death, but will willingly die for his master'.

ABOVE Historiated initial A. Passional, Germany, *c*.1170–1180. (BL HARLEY 2801 F. 7V)

OPPOSITE The royal arms of England of Henry VII, supported by a dragon and greyhound. Le Miroir des Dames. Manuscript dated to 1428, France. This illumination was added during the reign of Henry VII. (BL ROYAL 19 B XVI F. 1V)

VIVE LE NOBLE ROY HENRY

Using the image of a dog can also be a visual reference or pun on the bearer's own name. In the illumination on the left, John Talbot, 1st Earl of Shrewsbury, a leading English commander in the Hundred Years War, presents a book of romances to Margaret of Anjou, wife of Henry VI. A white dog stands in the foreground. The dog is a talbot, a large white hunting hound, shown here rather smaller than its actual scale.

ABOVE Lancelot in conversation with a lady. Estoire del Saint Graal, France, *c.*1315–*c.*1325.
(BL ROYAL 14 E III F. 146R)

OPPOSITE The Talbot Shrewsbury Book. Poems and Romances, France, *c.*1444–1445.
(BL ROYAL 15 E VI F. 2V)

Nearly all mentions of dogs in the Bible have negative connotations and are usually associated with cadavers. The only positive story relating to dogs is in the Book of Tobit: Tobit's son, Tobias, takes his dog with him when searching for a cure for his father's blindness. The dog appears in nearly all iconographic representations of Tobias.

ABOVE Tobit being cured. The Maastricht Hours, The Netherlands, *c.*1300–1325. (BL STOWE 17 F. 135R)

OPPOSITE Tobias, with his dog, and the archangel Raphael pointing to the fish. (BL ROYAL 15 D I F. 23R)

Alors se rapaisa la feme thobie.

Du graunt poysson qui
hurta le petit thobie par

uenti: ⁊ angl's dn̄i coartan

Fiat uia illoȝ tenebre ⁊ l

⁊ angelus domini pseque

Quoniam gratis abscon

michi interitum laquei su

Dog names were very varied in the Middle Ages. Nicholas Litlyngton, a fourteenth-century abbot of Westminster, had a dog named Sturdy. There are many different names inscribed on the collars of dogs in funeral effigies: Jakke (on the effigy of Sir Brian de Stapleton at Ingham, Norfolk), Bo (on an effigy of a member of the De Reynes family in Clifton Reynes, Buckinghamshire), Parceval and Dyamant (on the effigy of Jehan de Seure and his lady, Ozouer-le-Repos, Seine-et-Marne) and Terri, a shortened form of terrier, on a dog collar on the brass of Sir John Cassy's wife Alice (at Deerhurst, Gloucestershire). Two other names associated with types of dogs appear in a line in Chaucer's *The Nun's Priest's Tale*: 'Ran Colle oure dogge, and Talbot and Gerland' (a reference to the herding collie and white talbot hound. Gerland was a dog's personal name).

A list of 1,100 suitable names for hunting dogs is appended to an early fifteenth-century manuscript of *The Master of Game*, listing suggestions such as Nosewise, Swepestake, Smylfeste, Trynket, Amiable, Nameles, Holdfast and Absolom. A manuscript of *The Sayings of the Good Dog Souillard* lists appropriate names for hounds, such as Blonde and Blondeau, Rose and Roseau, Mirre and Mirau, Huielle and Huiiau, Ride and Rideau, Ribe and Ribau, Clincque and Clinqua, Bert and Berteau, Blesse and Blessiau, Oyse and Oyseau, Bride and Brideau.

OPPOSITE The Gorleston Psalter, England, 1310–1324. (BL ADD. 49622 F. 45R)

There were many legends about cynocephali, dog-headed people who lived in far-off lands. A story about St Andrew and St Bartholomew visiting the Parthians talks of a dog-headed man called 'Abominable' who lived in a city of cannibals (and lost his dog-head once baptised). There is an old tradition of St Christopher being a cynocephalus: Walter of Speyer (967–1027) portrayed him as a barking dog-headed cannibal. After meeting the Christ child, St Christopher repented, received baptism and then devoted himself to the service of God. The ninth-century theologian Ratramnus debated in a letter about whether the cynocephali should be seen as human or not. Marco Polo said that the cynocephali lived on Angamanain island (the Andaman Islands), while according to *The Travels of Sir John de Mandeville* they lived on Nacumera island.

OPPOSITE The cynocephali on Nacumera island. Sir John Mandeville, Travels, England, *c.*1425–1450. (BL HARLEY 3954 F. 41R)

[illegible] honouryn [illegible] and þ[illegible]
beryn a gret targe wt whyche þei coueryn al her body. And
a spere in her hand. And if þei takyn ony man in bataile þei send h[ym]
to here kyng. Whyche is a gret lord & a deuout in hys feyth.
he hath abowtyn hys necke on a corde .ccc. perlys gret & ori[ent]
in maner of pater nostris. And he seyth .ccc. preyers to hys god
eche day er he ete.

St Roch, the patron-saint of plague, is associated with a dog. According to his hagiography, he became famished after being thrown out of town because he was infected with the plague. In a forest he encountered a dog holding a loaf of bread in its mouth. The dog gave him the bread and licked his plague buboes. The dog's owner, a nobleman called Gothard, noticed how every day his dog came to the dinner table, took a loaf of bread in his mouth and then left the hall with it. One day Gothard set a very fine white loaf on the table which the dog took. He followed his dog to the forest and witnessed St Roch eating the bread. From that moment, Gothard supplied St Roch with food and anything else he needed.

When the mother of St Dominic (1170–1221) was pregnant, she dreamed of a black-and-white dog with a flaming torch in its mouth. The story symbolizes St Dominic's order guarding against the perils of heresy like watchful hounds, and elucidates the pun on the Dominicans: *domini canes* ('dogs of the Lord'). A similar story is told about St Bernard of Clairvaux (1090–1153), whose mother dreamt of a barking white dog when pregnant. This prefigured her son's vocation as a preacher who would bark against the enemies of the Church.

OPPOSITE An angel points to a plague bubo on St Roch's leg, as the dog holds the bread. Prayerbook of Joanna of Ghistelles, Netherlands, *c.*1516 (before 1529).
(BL EGERTON 2125 F. 209V)

The thirteenth-century preacher Stephen of Bourbon discovered, in the diocese of Lyons, a cult to an unofficial dog saint named Guinfort. Women were taking their children to the dog's forest shrine, as the dog saint was said to be a protector of the young. The locals would also pray to Guinfort when sick or in need of assistance. The preacher was told a story, which appears in different guises in many traditions. In this version, a local lord's baby had been left alone in the house. A giant snake appeared and came near the cradle. Guinfort, the lord's greyhound, attacked the snake and killed it, knocking over the cradle in the fight. When the lord and lady returned, they saw the cradle empty and Guinfort covered in blood. Assuming that the dog had killed the baby, the lord slew Guinfort with his sword. Shortly after, he discovered the baby asleep and the dead snake next to it. With great remorse, Guinfort's owner buried the dog and planted trees around the site, which then became the shrine discovered by Stephen of Bourbon.

OPPOSITE Margaret of York prays to the Risen Christ. Dialogue of the Duchess of Burgundy with Christ, Flanders, *c.*1470. (BL ADD. 7970 F. IV)

העולם בורא מאורי

In a thirteenth-century exemplary tale, a bishop of Paris, in a Solomonic decision, mediated between two clerics who both asserted that they were the owner of a dog. The first cleric claimed that the second had stolen his pet. After observing the dog, the bishop granted the dog to the thieving cleric, as the disputed dog obeyed him and responded to the name given by the thief, rather than his original owner.

ABOVE Scholar sits on bench with leashed dog. Pentateuch with the Five Scrolls and Haftarot, Germany, 1390–1396. (BL ADD. 19776 F. 54V)

OPPOSITE Hybrid pig-creature holds the First Cup for the Seder. Hare touches dog with stick. Haggadah, Spain, *c.*1340. (BL ADD. 14761 F. 26V)

The twelfth-century writer Walter Map, in his *On the Frivolities of Courtiers*, recounted the legend of the ancient King Herla, who was invited by a dwarf to a wedding and given a small hunting dog on his departure. The dwarf told Herla that he should hold the dog in his arms and that he and his men should not dismount until the dog had leapt away. When Herla returned to his kingdom, he discovered that hundreds of years had passed while he was in the dwarf's company. One of his knights tried to dismount but immediately died. Thus Herla and his men were condemned to wander around England forever, as the dog never left his arms.

ABOVE Shepherd and dog watching rams (for the zodiacal sign Aries). Calendar scene for March. The Queen Mary Psalter, England, *c.*1310–*c.*1320. (BL ROYAL 2 B VII F. 74R)

OPPOSITE Couple out riding. The Maastricht Hours, The Netherlands, *c.*1300–1325. (BL STOWE 17 F. 106R)

omnia mandata tua
dirigebar: omnẽ ui
am iniq̄m odio ha
bui. Gloria patri.

The late fourteenth-century author of the *Goodman of Paris* noted how

a greyhound, mastiff or little dog, whether on the road, or at table, or in bed, always stays close to the person who gives him food and ignores all others, being distant and shy with them. Even if far away, the dog always has his master in his heart. Even if his master whips or throws stones at the dog, the dog will still follow him, wagging his tail and lying down in front of his master to placate him. The dog will follow the master through rivers, woods, thieves and battles.

ABOVE Calendar scene for January. Book of Hours, Netherlands, *c.*1500. (BL EGERTON 1147 F. 6V)

OPPOSITE Harvesting. Calendar scene for August. The Golf Book. Hours of the Virgin, Flanders, sixteenth century. (BL ADD. 24098 F. 25V)

Fifteenth-century books of courtesy claimed that it was not well-mannered to stroke and feed dogs at the table. The thirteenth-century scholar Albertus Magnus, in his book *On Animals*, noted how giving dogs food from your plate made for poor guard dogs. 'The most ignoble genus of dogs before one's table are those that are thought to be on guard but which frequently so place themselves that they keep one eye on the door and one on the generous hand of the master.' Similarly, according to Albertus, a dog constantly petted by people makes a poor hunter as it then 'follows the track of those whom it loves'.

ABOVE Book of Hours, France, *c.*1325–1350. (BL ADD. 36684 F. 117R)

OPPOSITE The Last Supper. Book of Hours, Flanders, late fifteenth century. (BL ADD. 17280 F. 96V)

The fourteenth-century poet and scholar Francesco Petrarch (1304–1374) loved dogs and kept several as pets. He was given dogs by friends and patrons, and on one occasion adopted one that had been left at a house in which he was staying. He wrote profusely on the loyal nature of dogs and how he would walk around the countryside in the company of his faithful pet, or write with it sleeping nearby.

Dogs were principally fed bread in the Middle Ages, which medieval accounts usually call *panes pro canibus* ('bread for dogs'). The bread could be made from wheat and other grains. Porridge was another popular food, made either from oats, bran mash or barley, sometimes with added peas.

The Prioress, Madame Eglentyne, in Chaucer's Prologue to *The Canterbury Tales*, feeds her dogs meat, milk and very fine bread:

> Of small hounds had she that she fed
> With roasted flesh, or milk and wastel-bread.

Such a fine diet could, however, have dire consequences. Albertus Magnus wrote how ladies' lapdogs 'nearly always die of constipation' due to their over-indulgent diet. He recommended a regime of porridge to cure them.

OPPOSITE The Disputation of Saint Barbara. Book of Hours, France, fifteenth century. (BL ADD. 38126 F. 145V)

A gifte is doublid / whan it is youe soone

The fourteenth-century Dominican preacher John Bromyard described how pet dogs devoured food that their rich and uncaring masters and mistresses could have provided for the poor:

> The wealthy provide for their dogs more readily than for the poor, more abundantly and more delicately too; so that, whereas the poor are so famished that they would greedily devour bran-bread, dogs turn up their noses at the sight of wafer-bread, and spurn what is offered to them, trampling it under their feet. They must be offered the daintiest flesh, the first and choicest portion of every dish. If full, they refuse it. Then there is wailing about them, as though they were ill.

OPPOSITE St Edmund out hunting. John Lydgate, Metrical lives of Saints Edmund and Fremund, England, 1434–1439.
(BL HARLEY 2278 F. 37R)

Geoffroy de la Tour-Landry wrote a manual of instruction for his daughters in the fourteenth century, which included an exemplary tale of a pet owner suffering divine punishment due to spoiling her dogs (and neglecting the poor). The lady had two little dogs which she loved; she took great pleasure in their company and in feeding them meat and milk sop. A friar told her it was wrong that her dogs were so fat on such a diet, while there were so many thin and hungry poor people. The lady ignored his words and as she lay dying, two little black demonic dogs were seen on her bed, licking her mouth until it was as black as coal by the time she died.

OPPOSITE King David, with his harp and hound. Book of Hours, France, *c*.1460. (BL HARLEY 5762 F. 88R)

omine ne in fu
rore tuo arguas

la ou li veneour q les cacent les
tienent si cours que il se desesperoi
re et ne quide que iames puisse
son cors garandir. Il recourt arie
re courant batant cele part ou li
veneres vient por mourir devant
lui plus legierement. Des chiens.

Chiens naist non voians. mes
puis recevre sa veue selonc

The thirteenth-century scholar Albertus Magnus wrote extensively on canine care. Regarding puppies, he said that the best pup will be the last one to open its eyes or the one which the mother first carries. A pregnant bitch, he said, should be fed milk, whey, and butter with a little bread and cooked meat. He recommended feeding puppies whey mixed with buttery milk, and then weaning them at eight months on bread softened with a little whey. Under this regime they will be healthy within a year. Training for hunting should start once the dogs are a year and a half old, and they should be exposed to exercise gradually. To train a guard dog, it should be encouraged to attack a man covered in advance with thick hide (which the dog cannot tear). The man should fall down and let the dog bite him. Guard dogs, according to Albertus, should be tied and locked up all day, and only released at night.

OPPOSITE Breeds of dogs. At bottom right, bitch with puppies. Brunetto Latini, Li Livres dou Tresor, France, c.1315–1325. (BL YATES THOMPSON 19 F. 60V)

Common diseases of dogs listed by Albertus Magnus included skin diseases such as impetigo and scabies (cured with bleeding and using an ointment made from mercury, sulphur, nettle seeds and lard or butter). Spines or thorns in paws or fur could be pulled out after applying a mixture of bran and lard to the affected area. Fleas could be removed with olive oil. If a dog was too thin, it should be fed a lot of butter.

The early fifteenth-century treatise *The Master of Game* by Edward, Duke of York (mostly a translation of Gaston Phoebus's *Livre de la chasse*) suggested an ointment of leeks, garlic, chives and rue to apply to dogs bitten by other dogs (along with cupping the wound) and assorted remedies for mange. For 'quick' mange (skin broken in many places) he gave an ointment recipe of honey, verdigris, nut oil, water and valerian leaf. For 'flying' mange (mange around the ears and legs), an ointment of mercury, the saliva of fasting men and pig grease. For 'common' mange (in which dogs scratch and bite themselves) he suggested anointing the dog with a mixture of iris, nut oil, water, black pitch and rosin.

OPPOSITE Dives, feasting, on the far right, as the leprous Lazarus approaches. Book of Hours, France, *c.*1500. (BL YATES THOMPSON 5 F. 70V)

DILEXI qm exaudiet do
minus : uoce orônis me
Qua inclinauit aurem suam m
chi : et in diebz meis inuocabo
Circundederunt me dolores mo

LORIA·IN·NES·EX

The Master of Game recounted that for a dog's eye disease which caused a web on the eye and 'flesh on one side of the eye called a nail', some men placed an elm-branch collar around the dog. He instead recommended rubbing the juice of greater celandine, ginger powder, and pepper (!) into the dog's eye, taking care that the dog did not rub it. If this was not possible, surgery with a needle could be attempted. For afflictions in the ears, when dogs claw their ears and 'out of her ears comes much foul things, and some time thereafter they become deaf', he suggested washing the inside of the ears with lukewarm wine, and then putting in drops of oil and camomile juice. For *malemort* in the nostrils (glanders), when the dog could smell nothing, one should boil mastic, incense, water, calamint, nigella, rue, mint and sage. The dog should then inhale this steaming mixture.

OPPOSITE Annunciation to the Shepherds. Book of Hours, France, sixteenth century. (BL ADD. 31240 F. 62R)

If a dog could not keep down any food, *The Master of Game* said 'the best medicine is to let them go wherever they will, and let them eat all that ever they will'. They should be given finely cut meat put in broth or goat's milk, and in small portions. If any limb was out of joint or broken, they should be put back into joint, and flax moistened with egg-white placed on the afflicted area. If their paw-pads were bruised due to running on stones or hard ground, they should be washed with water and salt. To avoid injury to claws, dogs should have them neatly clipped.

ABOVE Hare plays portable organ, dog plays bagpipes. The Breviary of Renaud de Bar, France, *c.*1302–3. (BL YATES THOMPSON 8 F. 184V)

OPPOSITE Charles the Bold receives Vasco da Lucena's translation of Quintus Curtius. Quinte Curce Ruffe des fais du grant Alexandre, Flanders, *c.*1468. (BL ROYAL 20 C III F. 12R)

Treshault tres
puissant et tres
excellent prince
et mon tresre-
doubte seigneur
Charles par la grace de dieu
duc de bourgoingne de lothric
de brabant de lembourg et
de luxembourg Conte de
flandres dartois de bourg
Palatin de haynnau de hol-
lande de zeellande de namur
et cetera Vasque de lucene
portugalois humble serviteur
et prompte obeissance tout
temps avecque voulente me
prent de assambler et trans-
later de latin en francois

Galliric

Nomen herbe
Alii Sangui-
nariã uocant.
Nascitur locis soli-
dis & circa uias.
Ad morsũ canis.
Herbã Gallicrus.
teris cũ axungia &
pane domestico & po-
nis mox sanabit' item
& duritias discutit.
Ut sanguis de naribus
currat. Herbã Sanguina-
riã sũ naribꝫ mittis continuo
sanguinẽ mira celeritate emittit
& caput leuiorẽ facit.

xl

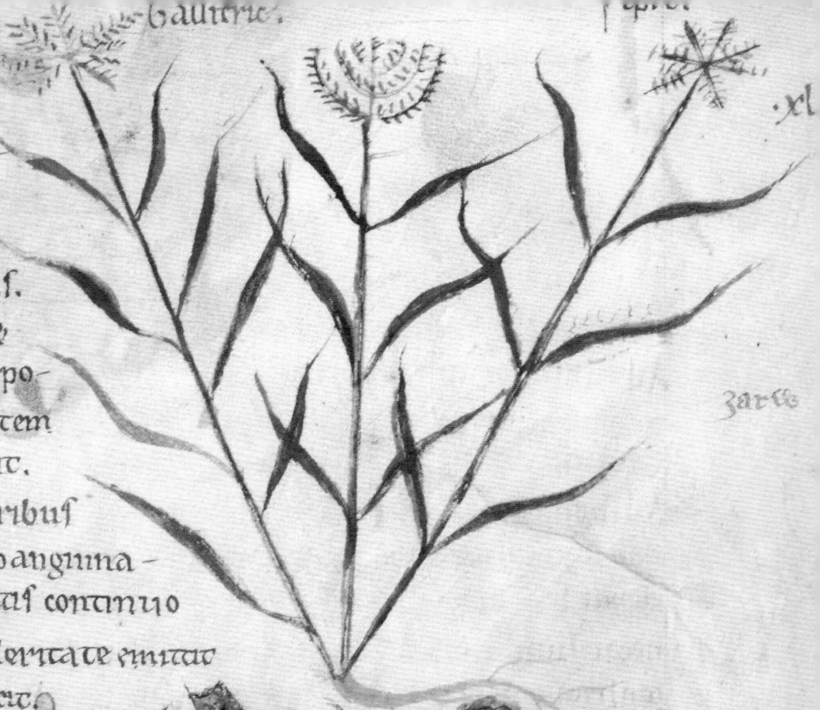

Rabies was a feared and deadly disease, and it was known that it could be transmitted to humans via a dog bite. In addition to remedies for the afflicted patient, there were also remedies for dogs. The French surgeon Henri de Mondeville (*c.*1260–*c.*1320) claimed that the best cure was bathing any rabid dog (or person) nine times in sea water. He remarked that in his native Normandy it was common to see dogs being taken to the seashore for curative sea-bathing, and how docile they were after the treatment. Albertus Magnus suggested adding hen's faeces to the dog's food. He also informed his readers of another cure, that of immersing a rabid dog in warm water for nine days, with its front legs raised up and its back legs hardly touching the bottom. Once removed from the water, the dog should be shaved all over and covered in beet juice at frequent intervals. Any food given to the dog should be covered with the same juice. If the dog did not recover after seven days, it would need to be killed.

OPPOSITE A rabid dog bites a man's leg. Pseudo-Apuleius and other medical texts, England, *c.*1150–1200. (BL HARLEY 5294 F. 25R)

The tradition of the apparition of mysterious black dogs is a long one. *The Anglo-Saxon Chronicle* recounts that when Henry of Poitou arrived in Peterborough to take up his post as abbot, many men saw and heard, in the nearby deer park and woods, a pack of black huntsmen on black horses and on black goats, accompanied by terrifying black dogs with huge eyes.

ABOVE Lothbrok in a boat, with hound. John Lydgate, Metrical lives of Saints Edmund and Fremund, England, 1434–1439. (BL HARLEY 2278 F. 41V)

OPPOSITE Lothbrok hunting. John Lydgate, Metrical lives of Saints Edmund and Fremund, England, 1434–1439. (BL HARLEY 2278 F. 43V)

And thouh lothbrocus / were of hih estat
In his contre / and of gret excellence
Yit in such game / he was most fortunat
And therof hadde / famous experience
Thoruh whos besy / waker dilligence
His hauk and he / took foules many fold
Ech day them brouhte / hoom to the housshold

Al watir foul / and foul upon the lond
Wher he fond plente / in any maner place
Ther myht noon escape / from his hond
And beestis wilde / ful weel he koude enchace
And thus he stood weel / in the kynges grace
Eek al the housshold / gan hym magnefie
Sauf Bern the hunte hadde at hym envye

[illegible]
la misericorde dieu pdurablemēt
Je regehirai a toy pdurablemēt
pource que tu las fait et atendrai
ton nom pource quil est bons ou
regart de ses sains.
Dixit insipiens in corde suo
non est deus. psalmus dauid.

[illegible]
Qui donrra de syon
isrl'. quāt mesires dest
chetiuoison de son p
leescera iacob et esiour
Deus in nomin
me fac et in uirtute
ca me. ps dd
Diex en moy sa
et me iuge en t
Diex oies moroison
par oreilles les paro
che.
Pource que estra
esdrecie contre moy. e
stirent mame. et ne p
dieu deuant son regar
Estes vo' diex ai
us est recueilleres de m
Sur tourne maul

Ghostly dogs occur in Giovanni Boccaccio's fourteenth-century *Decameron*, when the ghost of Guido degli Anastagi and his dogs track down and kill a woman who had rejected him and caused his suicide.

ABOVE Entertainer in a bishop costume with a performing dog. The Luttrell Psalter, England, c.1325–1335. (BL ADD. 42130 F. 84R)

OPPOSITE A fool with his bauble, loaf and dog, for Psalm 52 (Vulgate). Bible historiale, France, 1357. (BL ROYAL 17 E VII F. 241R)

Dog collars in the Middle Ages were usually made of leather or cloth, and lapdogs often wore collars covered in little tinkling bells. In an inventory of goods belonging to Charles V of France in 1380 there are many luxury dog collars:

Item, a collar of silver, with bells for a little dog.

Item, a very small dog collar of blue cloth, with a gold fleur-de-lys and three gold bells, with a gold buckle.

Item, thirteen collars, for hounds and other dogs, made of silver.

Item, a hound collar made of silver, which the Duc de Berry gave to the queen Jehanne de Bourbon.

A small baton of ivory, to admonish dogs.

A blue velvet dog collar, decorated with silver.

A collar for a hound with gold studs, and a fleur-de-lys on each stud.

OPPOSITE Christine de Pisan presents her book to Isabeau of Bavaria. Christine de Pisan, Various works, France, *c.*1410–*c.*1414. (BL HARLEY 4431 F. 3R)

Tres excellent de grant haultesse
Couronnee puissant princesse
Tresnoble Royne de france
Le corps enclin vers vous madresse
En saluant par grant hūblesse

Dogs could sleep in kennels or baskets, on the floor and even on beds, as attested by the fourteenth-century poet John Gower when describing his mistress's bedroom:

> I play with her little hound
> Now on the bed, now on the ground.

In Gottfried von Strassburg's thirteenth-century romance *Tristan*, Isolde has a kennel made for Petitcreiu, the magical little lapdog. It is made of gold and precious stones, with a blanket of brocade for the dog to sleep on.

Richard II's greyhound Math abandoned his master once he had been deposed by Henry of Lancaster (Henry IV). Math ignored his old master, and sought the new king's favour, which Henry saw as a favourable sign, letting Math sleep on his bed.

OPPOSITE Job with his family. Hours of the Virgin, France, early sixteenth century. (BL ADD. 35215 F. 98V)

Many monasteries and nunneries tried to stop dogs being kept by monks and nuns. Walter of Wenlock, Abbot of Westminster, ordered his household not to keep dogs or birds. When William Alnwick, Bishop of Lincoln, visited Daventry Priory in 1442 he complained that all the monks kept dogs, to which they gave the leftovers that should have been destined for the poor. William Greenfield, Archbishop of York, remonstrated in 1314–15 about the practice of bringing little dogs into the choir during divine services as this would 'impede the service and hinder the devotion of the nuns'. Similarly, Hugo Seton, Archdeacon of Ely, in 1345 forbade the nuns of Chatteris and Icketon from having dogs as pets, and from keeping them under the choir bench. William of Wykeham, Bishop of Winchester, in 1387 compromised with the nuns of Romsey, Wherwell and St Mary's, Winchester: although keeping pets in the nunnery would not be prohibited, the nuns were forbidden from bringing them into the church itself. They would have to suffer a one-day bread and water fast if they disobeyed his orders.

OPPOSITE Page from an unfinished genealogical work on the Royal Houses of Spain and Portugal, Flanders, early sixteenth century. (BL ADD. 12531 F. 4R)

RISTA
RA DON

It was not always nuns, however, that caused problems in the nunneries. A prioress of Langley in 1440 complained about a lady resident: 'Lady Audley, who is boarding here, has a great many dogs, so many that when she comes to church, her twelve dogs follow, who make great noise in church, stopping the nuns in their psalms, and by this, the nuns are terrified.'

ABOVE Nun holding a dog. The Maastricht Hours, The Netherlands, *c.*1300–1325. (BL STOWE 17 F. 100R)

OPPOSITE The fortress of faith, surrounded by the fathers of the Church. A dog chases a mallard duck. Alphonsus de Spina, translated by Pierre Richard, La forteresse de la foy, France and Netherlands, *c.*1475–1500. (BL ROYAL 17 F VI–VII F. 146R)

Ordinances made at Eltham in 1526 during the reign of Henry VIII state:

The King's Highness alsoe forbiddeth and inhibiteth, that no person whatsoever he be, presume to keep any grey-hounds, mastiffs, hounds, or other than some few small spaniels for ladies or others, nor bring or lead any into the same, except it be by the King's or the Queen's commandment; but the said grey-hounds and doggs to be kept in kennels, and other meet places, out of court, as it is convenient, so as, the premises duly observed, the house may be sweet, wholesome, cleane, and well furnished, as to a prince's honour and estate doth appertain.

ABOVE A hare rides a dog. John le Breton, The Treatise on the Laws of England, England, c.1305. (BL HARLEY 324 F. 3V)

OPPOSITE Simon de Hesdin presents his book to Charles V. Valerius Maximus, translated by Simon de Hesdin and Nicholas de Gonesse, Les Fais et les Dis des Romains et de autres gens, Netherlands, 1475–1500. (BL HARLEY 4430 F. 33R)

commence le livre de valere le grant translate de latin en
religieuse personne. Maistre simon de hesdin maistre
ne. Et frere de saint Jehan de Iherusalem Et commence
briefte et
fragilite de
ceste dolereuse
vie linconsta
aussi de la voulente
pensee humaine son
cause. pourquoy len
fait a ce commencem

Namque pedes subter rutilo cum lumine claret
Feruidus ille canis stellarum luce refulgens
Hunc tegit obscurus subter praecordia uertex
At uero toto spirans de corpore flammam
Aestifero rabidus erumpit flatibus ignes.
Totus ab ore micans iacitur mortalibus ardor.
His ubi se pariter cum sole in lumina caeli
Extulit. haud patitur foliorum tegmine frustra
Suspensos animos arbusta ornata tenere.
Nam quorum stirpis tellus amplexa prehendit
Haec augens anima uitali flamina mulcet.
At quorum nequeunt radices findere terras.
Denudat foliis ramos. et cortice truncos.

SYRIUS

In astronomical manuscripts, the two canine constellations, Canis Major (Larger Dog) and Canis Minor (Smaller Dog), companions of the constellation of the hunter Orion, are often depicted. Sirius, the 'dog-star', a binary-star and the brightest in the sky, is represented by either the nose or the tongue in Canis Major in these two illuminations.

Since ancient times Sirius was believed to be responsible for hot late summer days and the diseases that often occurred at the same time, along with making dogs go mad.

ABOVE The constellation Canis Major. The Aratea (astronomical poem by Aratus of Soli, translated by Marcus Tullius Cicero as the Phaenomena), France, *c.*975–1000. (BL HARLEY 2506 F. 44V)

OPPOSITE Illustration of Sirius as the tongue of Canis Major. The Aratea, France, ninth century. (BL HARLEY 647 F. 8V)

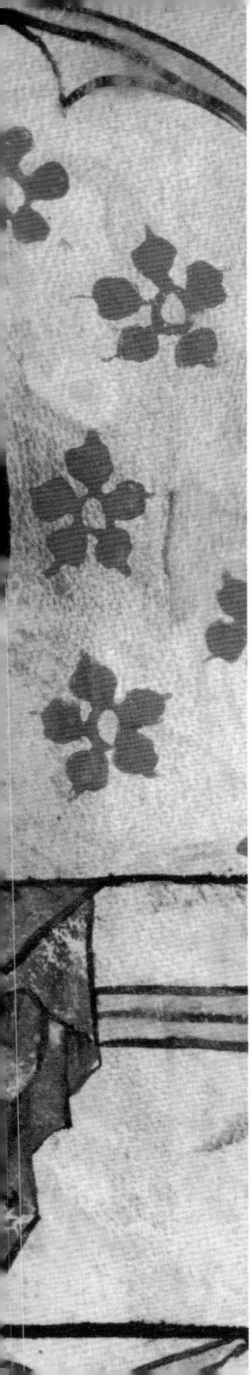

In Guillaume Machaut's fourteenth-century *The Judgement of the King of Behaigne* the narrator uses a hostile pet dog as a means of introduction to a lady:

When I had come so near them that I could see them quite clearly and openly, the little dog, which didn't know me at all, began to yelp. I noticed that the lady, who well understood proper behaviour, was startled and called to it. But the dog paid very little heed to her call; he approached me barking and sunk his teeth into my robe. I grabbed him and, in his fright, he stopped barking. In my heart I was delighted to bring him back to his mistress, for it gave me the opportunity and occasion to go where I wished; therefore I kept stroking his coat.

OPPOSITE Brutus, founder of Britain, and Innogent. Peter of Langtoft's Chronicle, England, *c.*1307–1327. (BL ROYAL 20 A II F. 2R)

In Chaucer's *The Book of the Duchess*, the narrator encounters a small dog as he wanders:

I was gone walking from my tree
And as I went there came by me
A whelp, that fawned upon me as I stood
That had followed but was untrained.
It came and crept up to me as lowly
Right as if it had known me
Held down its head and joined its ears
And laid its ears' hair down all smooth.

ABOVE Detail from calendar scene for October. The Golf Book. Hours of the Virgin, Flanders, sixteenth century. (BL ADD. 24098 F. 27V)

OPPOSITE Lovers in a garden. Calendar scene for April. The Golf Book. Hours of the Virgin, Flanders, sixteenth century. (BL ADD. 24098 F. 21V)

Afftir the grehound the knyht than folwe a paas
Most secrely and maad therof no tale
By whom he kam there as lothbrocus was
Hid vnder leues in a couert vale
His wounde bloody his face ded and pale
His eyen gastlewh reuersid bothe tweyne
His hound a side which dide his deth compleyne

Moordre wil out thouh it a bide a while
Lyk his decert he must receyue his meede
ffor of this treson and fals compassid gyle
The venymous roote began first of hatreede
ffor it was founde that Bern hath doon this deede
By certeyn signes and for to make a preeff
To knowe the trouthe the grehound was most cheeff

In the ninth century, St Edmund, King of East Anglia, entertained Ragnarr Lothbrok, king of Zealand and Uppsala. When out hunting Lothbrok was killed by the king's huntsman, one Bjorn. Bjorn hid the body in the bushes and returned home, but Lothbrok's faithful greyhound remained at his slain master's side. When Edmund asked about Lothbrok's whereabouts, Bjorn replied that he was behind him in the wood. At that very moment the greyhound appeared and wagged its tail. Assuming that Lothbrok must be still hunting, the dog was fed but it soon left (going back to the body). It returned home three days later, famished, and was then followed back to Lothbrok's body. Another version of the story has Lothbrok captured by King Aella of Northumbria who throws him into a pit of vipers.

ABOVE Lothbrok's hound returns home without his master. John Lydgate, Metrical lives of Saints Edmund and Fremund, England, 1434–1439. (BL HARLEY 2278 F. 44V)

OPPOSITE Lothbrok's body is discovered. (BL HARLEY 2278 F. 45V)

The popular herbal of Pseudo-Apuleius gives instructions for uprooting a mandrake plant, which was said to scream in the process (and hearing this would kill a man): first you dig around it with an iron implement, taking care not to touch the plant. Then, when you see the 'hands and feet' (the roots of the plant were said to resemble a man), you tie them with some rope and tie the rope to a hungry dog's neck. You then place some meat in front of the dog, but out of its reach. That way you can safely be out of hearing of the screaming mandrake plant as the dog uproots the plant in its effort to get to the meat.

ABOVE Ladies in a carriage: one receives a pet dog, another stands with a pet squirrel on her shoulder. A dog walks underneath. The Luttrell Psalter, England, *c*.1325–1335.
(BL ADD. 42130 F. 181V)

OPPOSITE The Annunciation to the Shepherds. Book of Hours, France, *c*.1400–1450.
(BL ADD. 32454 F. 32R)

Adoncques incon-
tinent se soubz-
mistrent tous
a la premiere voix dalixandre
et lui presenterent un tyrant
chien lequel estoit si fort
que en la presence dalixandre
il vainqui un lyon et un
olifant. Atant se parti le
roy alixandre darbanie et
retourna par partie de
campie et de la entra en
la terre dinde laquelle il

murmuroit et
cause car tous
serons en plo
ensemble et deso
maniere suffi
et que nous avo
en perse et de
avons plusieurs
soubzmises en
et ainsi alons
paix et voulons
guerre inde ou
ne sont fors

In Sextus Placitus's late antique book of medicines made from animals, he gives the following remedies: to make sure dogs do not bother you or bark at you, carry the heart of a dog; the ashes of a dog's head, drunk in wine, will cure anyone bitten by a rabid dog; and the head of the rabid dog which bites you, if cooked and eaten, will cure you.

ABOVE A crane bites a dog in an initial E. Geoffrey of Monmouth's Historia regum Britanniae and other texts, England, *c.*1294. (BL EGERTON 3142 F. 14R)

OPPOSITE Albanians present Alexander the Great with a dog which can fight elephants. Le Livre et le vraye hystoire du bon roy Alixandre, France, *c.*1420. (BL ROYAL 20 B XX F. 41V)

When the beloved dog of Thierry, Abbot of St Thrond, died in the late eleventh or early twelfth century, his master commemorated the little dog in an elegy as:

the chief concern and grief of his master. He was not a large dog… but a slight dog and short pup…he was five years old…modest he was in size.… White in colour, he bejewelled his face with black eyes. What was his function? Was it a useful one or not? That his large master should love a small dog – that was his duty, to play before his master. What was the use of that? There was none, if not laughter! No one failed to laugh at him as he stood or as he moved.… Such you were, beloved dog, to be laughed at and grieved; you were laughter while you were alive, but look at the grief when you have died! Whoever saw you, whoever knew you, loves you and grieves now over your demise, pitiable dog.

OPPOSITE King John and his dogs. Peter of Langtoft's Chronicle and other texts, England, *c.*1307–1327. (BL ROYAL 20 A II F. 8V)

Johannes Rex anglie genuit
Henricum Regem Anglie

l iure dedigit : gallis possessa u

Johannes rex genuit videlic

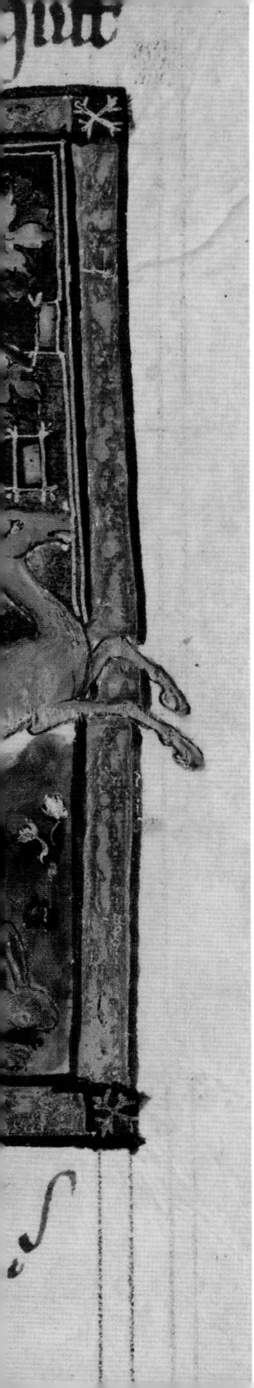

Edward, Duke of York, in his *Master of Game* discusses hunting dogs:

Now will I tell you of the nature of hounds which hunt...a hound is true to his lord or his master...a hound is of great understanding and of great knowledge, a hound has great strength and great bounty. A hound is a wise beast...has great mind and great smelling...a hound is of great worthiness...a hound is of good obedience, for he will learn as a man all that man will teach him, a hound is full of good sport... a hound will keep his master's house and his beasts and he will also keep all his mistress's goods, and would rather be dead than anything be lost in his keeping.

OPPOSITE King John stag-hunting. The Book of the Laws of Ancient Kings, England, *c*.1321.
(BL COTTON CLAUDIUS D II F. 116R)

The fifteenth-century *Boke of St Albans* lists 'the names of diverse manner of hounds', which are the greyhound, 'bastard' (greyhound cross), mongrel, mastiff, lymer, spaniel, 'rache' (running-hound), 'kenet' (small hunting-hound), terrier, butcher's hound, midden-dog, trundle-tail, prick-eared cur and small ladies' puppies that bear away the fleas.

The same text lists the properties of a good greyhound:

> A Greyhound should be headed like
> a snake
> And necked like a drake
> Footed like a cat
> Tailed like a rat
> Sided like a bream
> Chained like a beam.

OPPOSITE Soldiers pay homage to the emperor. Valerius Maximus, translated by Simon de Hesdin and Nicolas de Gonesse, Les Fais et les Dis des Romains et de autres gens, France, *c.*1460–1487. (BL HARLEY 4372 F. 182R)

En ceste par
et en lueure valerius dom
dit ainsi lacteur Je me tran

Qui operatus est pe
tro in apo sto la tum o
ratus est et michi inter
entes · Et cognouerunt gra

Pseudo-Albertus Magnus's *Book of the Virtues of Herbs, Stones and Animals* gives the following recipes: among the virtues of stones, lipparea (a stone from Libya) is greatly loved by wild beasts, as it lets neither dogs nor hunters hurt them; if a man places the heart and right foot of an owl under his armpit, no dog will bark at him; if a dog eats the heart, eyes and tongue of a weasel, then he will lose his voice; if a man binds the right eye of a wolf on his right sleeve neither men nor dogs can hurt him.

ABOVE A hare attacks a dog. The Gorleston Psalter, England, 1310–1324.
(BL 49622 F. 88R)

OPPOSITE A dog dances and sings. The Breviary of Renaud de Bar, France, *c*.1302–3
(BL YATES THOMPSON 8 F. 284R)

A treatise of medical and magical preparations from animals lists the following preparations from dogs:

The teeth of a dog carried (or bound around his arm or neck) by a patient with jaundice will cure him.

Dogs will not bark at you if you wear a dog's tooth. If you have a black dog's tooth in your palm, dogs will not bark at you, which is why it is carried by thieves.

The head of dog, burned to ashes and mixed with rose oil, should be applied on ulcers.

ABOVE Brackes (hunting hounds). Jacon van Maerlandt's Der Naturen Bloeme (translation of Thomas de Cantimpré's De natura rerum). Flanders, thirteenth century. (ADD. 11390 F. 8V)

OPPOSITE Dogs chase hares and another sits with a belled collar. Jacon van Maerlandt's Der Naturen Bloeme (translation of Thomas de Cantimpré's De natura rerum). Flanders, thirteenth century. (ADD. 11390 F. 8R)

niuf die meester togher
ens kemels ersine droghet
danne drinket met al sine
t soe sochtet die grote pine
iden ëuele darmen of vallet
lef vandien kemele ghevallet

anis dats in diersch en hont
iacob van vitri maket ons cont
t beesten sijn dien men mach wel
eren meneghe rande spel
t al slapē si gherne mede
chtan so est hare sede
t si thuus wachten voer den dief
ren here hebsi so lief
t si dicken doot sijn bleue
nne te bescermene hare here leue
t dies toghē si noch vele
chtes end al met haren ghebele

hont

Further Reading

PRIMARY SOURCES

John Caius, *Of Englishe Dogges: The Diversities, the Names, the Natures, and the Properties*, trans. A. Fleming (1578) [available online]

Edward, Duke of York, *The Master of Game* (London, 1904) [available online]

Albertus Magnus, *On Animals: A Medical Summa Zoologica*, ed. and trans. K.F. Kitchell and I.M. Resnick, vol.2 (Baltimore, 1999), quoted pp. 34 and 37

The Goodman of Paris, trans. E. Power (Woodbridge, 2006)

Guillaume Machaut, *Le Jugement dou Roy de Behainge*, ed. J.I. Wimsatt and W.W. Kibler (Athens, Georgia, 1988), quoted p. 69

SECONDARY SOURCES

G.G. Coulton, *Social Life in Britain from the Conquest to the Reformation* (Cambridge, 1918) [available online]

J. Cummins, *The Hound and the Hawk: The Art of Medieval Hunting* (London, 1988)

N.C. Flores, ed., *Animals in the Middle Ages* (New York, 1996)

L.A.J.R. Houwn, *The Deidis of Armorie: A Herdaldic Treatise and Bestiary* (Edinburgh, 1994)

S. Menache, 'Dogs: god's worst enemies?', *Society and Animals*, 5:1 (1997), pp. 23–44

S. Menache, 'Dogs and human beings: a story of friendship', *Society and Animals*, 6:1 (1998), pp. 67–86

B. Resl, *A Cultural History of Animals in the Middle Ages* (Oxford and New York, 2007)

B. Rowland, *Blind Beasts: Chaucer's Animal World* (Chatham, 1971)

B. Rowland, *Animals with Human Faces: A Guide to Animal Symbolism* (London, 1974)

J.E. Salisbury, *The Beast Within: Animals in the Middle Ages* (London, 1994)

J.-C. Schmitt, *The Holy Greyhound: Guinefort, Healer of Children Since the Thirteenth Century* (Cambridge and Paris, 1983)

J.A. Serpell, *In the Company of Animals* (Oxford, 1986)

M. Thiébaux, 'The medieval chase', *Speculum*, 42:2 (1967), pp. 260–74

K. Walker-Meikle, *Cats in Medieval Manuscripts* (London, 2019)

K. Walker-Meikle, *Medieval Pets* (Woodbridge, 2012)

J.M. Ziolkowski, *Talking Animals: Medieval Latin Beast Poetry, 750–1150* (Philadelphia, 1993), quoted p. 78

ONLINE SOURCES

Medieval Animal Data-Network
mad.imareal.sbg.ac.at

The Medieval Bestiary
bestiary.ca

COVER

Dogs fill the street between Dives and Lazarus. Book of Hours, France, *c.*1500
(BL YATES THOMPSON 5 F. 70V)

FRONTISPIECE

Creation of the animals and Initial C. The Maastricht Hours, The Netherlands, *c.*1300–1325
(BL STOWE 17 F. 24R AND F. 111R)

FRONT ENDPAPERS

Dogs play in the margins of the Hours of the Dead. Book of Hours, France, *c.*1325–1350
(BL ADD. 36684 F. 91V AND F. 90R)

BACK ENDPAPERS

A dog assists an organ-playing hare. The Gorleston Psalter, England, 1310–1324
(BL ADD. 49622 F. 138R)

A dog with a pipe and tabor. The Gorleston Psalter, England, 1310–1324
(BL ADD. 49622 F. 82R)

First published in 2013 by
The British Library
96 Euston Road
London NW1 2DB

This edition published in 2020

British Library Cataloguing-in-Publication Data
A catalogue record for this book is available from The British Library
ISBN 978 0 7123 5302 1

Designed and typeset by Andrew Barron
Colour reproduction by Dot Gradations Ltd
Printed in China by Great Wall Printing Co. Ltd

Note from the author: Many thanks to Reider Payne, Isobel Meikle, Alistair Walker, Mike Parker, David d'Avray, P.D.A. Harvey, and Sophie Page.

The spelling of many words in quoted Middle English texts has been modernized

Cito fecerunt obliti sunt operum eius:
et non sustinuerunt consilium eius.
Et concupierunt concupiscenciam in de-
serto: et temptaverunt deum in inaquoso.
Et dedit eis peticionem ipsorum: et misit
saturitatem in animas eorum.
Et irritaverunt moysen in castris:
aaron sanctum domini.
Aperta est terra et deglutivit dathan:
et operuit super congregacionem abyron.

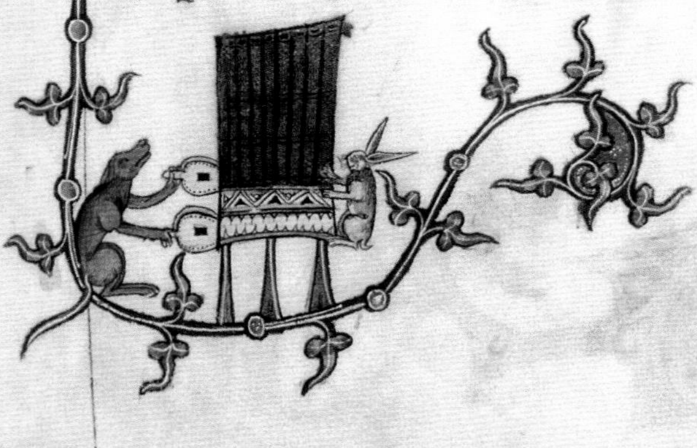